CHRISTIAN WEDDING Collection

25 CONTEMPORARY & TRADITIONAL SACRED SONGS

ISBN 978-1-4234-6312-2

HAL•LEONARD®
CORPORATION

7777 W. BLUEMOUND RD. P.O. BOX 13819 MILWAUKEE, WI 53213

Visit Hal Leonard Online at
www.halleonard.com

AVE MARIA

By CHARLES GOUNOD
based on "Prelude in C Major" by Johann Sebastian Bach

Andante con moto

BLESS THE BROKEN ROAD

Words and Music by MARCUS HUMMON,
BOBBY BOYD and JEFF HANNA

To Coda ⊕

AVE MARIA

By FRANZ SCHUBERT

CINDERELLA

Words and Music by
STEVEN CURTIS CHAPMAN

With a lilt

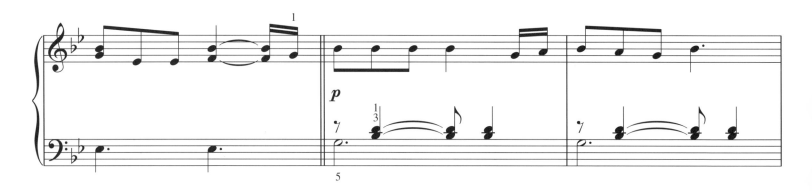

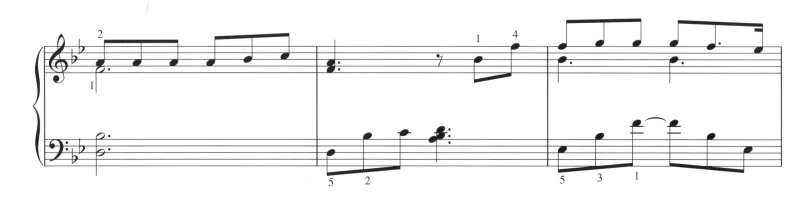

To Coda ✛

CROSS MY HEART

Words and Music by MICHAEL W. SMITH
and WAYNE KIRKPATRICK

Moderately

D.S. al Coda

CODA

GOD CAUSES ALL THINGS TO GROW

Words and Music by STEVEN CURTIS CHAPMAN
and STEVE GREEN

JESU, JOY OF MAN'S DESIRING

By JOHANN SEBASTIAN BACH

Moderato

HOUSEHOLD OF FAITH

Words by BRENT LAMB
Music by JOHN ROSASCO

HOW BEAUTIFUL

Words and Music by
TWILA PARIS

I WILL BE HERE

Words and Music by
STEVEN CURTIS CHAPMAN

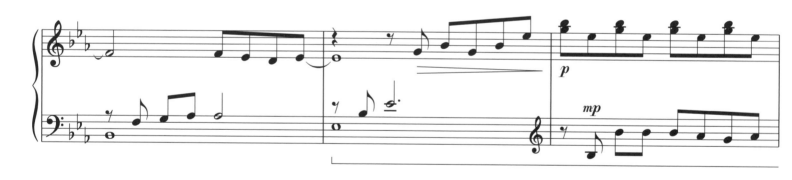

To Coda

D.S. al Coda

CODA

IF YOU COULD SEE WHAT I SEE

Words and Music by GEOFF MOORE
and STEVEN CURTIS CHAPMAN

JOYFUL, JOYFUL, WE ADORE THEE

Words by HENRY VAN DYKE
Music by LUDWIG VAN BEETHOVEN,
melody from *Ninth Symphony*

Brightly

LISTEN TO OUR HEARTS

Words and Music by GEOFF MOORE
and STEVEN CURTIS CHAPMAN

THE LANGUAGE OF JESUS IS LOVE

Words and Music by PHILL McHUGH,
GREG NELSON, SCOTT WESLEY BROWN
and PHIL NAISH

Slowly, with expression

THE LORD'S PRAYER

By ALBERT H. MALOTTE

Slowly, reverently

With pedal

Majestically, slightly brighter

LOVE WILL BE OUR HOME

Words and Music by
STEVEN CURTIS CHAPMAN

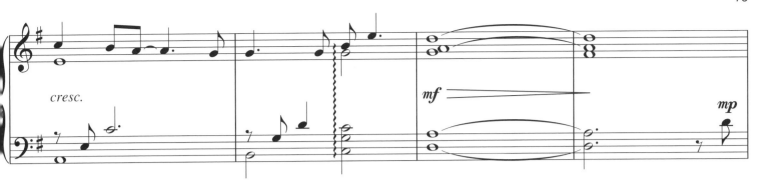

MAKE US ONE

Words and Music by
TWILA PARIS

Moderately slow, in 2

PANIS ANGELICUS
(O Lord Most Holy)

By CÉSAR FRANCK

WEDDING PRAYER

By FERN G. DUNLAP

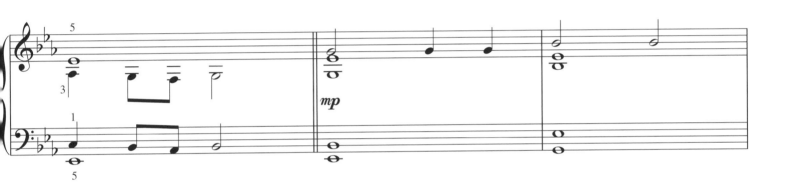

SEEKERS OF YOUR HEART

Words and Music by MELODIE TUNNEY,
DICK TUNNEY and BEVERLY DARNALL

SHINE ON US

Words and Music by MICHAEL W. SMITH
and DEBBIE SMITH

Steadily driving

THIS DAY

Words and Music by
LOWELL ALEXANDER

Moderately slow, expressively

To Coda

'TIL THE END OF TIME

Words and Music by
STEVE GREEN

Gently, in 2

mp

With pedal

mf

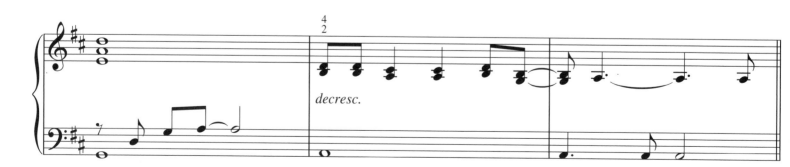

decresc.

WEDDING SONG
(There Is Love)

Words and Music by
PAUL STOOKEY

Moderately slow, in 2

mp

With pedal

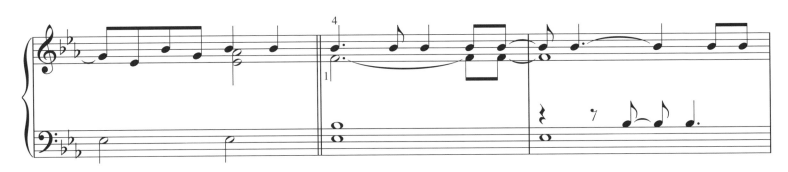

YOU RAISE ME UP

Words and Music by BRENDAN GRAHAM
and ROLF LOVLAND